C000038580

Royal Horticultural Society

Sharing the best in Gardening

PLANT NOTEBOOK

FRANCES LINCOLN LIMITED
PUBLISHERS

A Growing Society

Throughout its history the Royal Horticultural Society has inspired people to discover new and interesting plants and encouraged an interest in gardening. This RHS *Plant Notebook* is designed to help you keep notes on your own personal discoveries.

With its spectacular flower shows, world-class gardens and the highest standards in advice, science and education, the RHS is at the heart of gardening today. To become a member, all you need is an interest in gardening. One of the many benefits of membership is free access to our Garden Advice Service covering such queries as where to buy and how to grow plants, plant identification, pests and diseases and garden products.

For more information please call our membership hotline on 0845 1304646 or visit our website **www.rhs.org.uk**

CONTENTS

TREES

PLANT NAME	WHERE SEEN

SUPPLIER	PLANTING POSITION

PLANT NAME	WHERE SEEN

SUPPLIER	PLANTING POSITION

PLANT NAME	WHERE SEEN

SUPPLIER	PLANTING POSITION

PLANT NAME	WHERE SEEN

SUPPLIER	PLANTING POSITION

PLANT NAME	WHERE SEEN

SUPPLIER	PLANTING POSITION

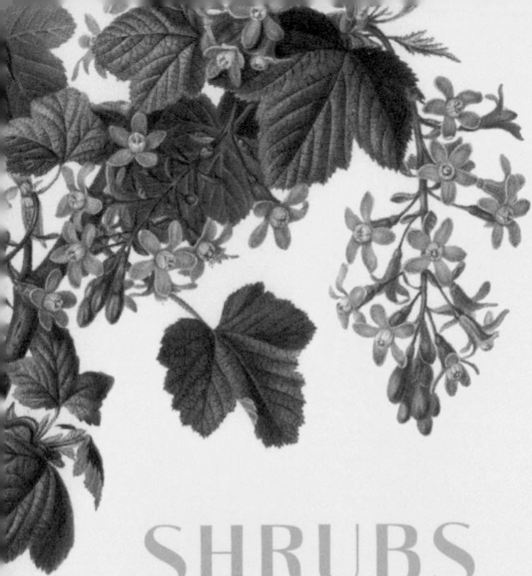

SHRUBS

PLANT NAME	WHERE SEEN

SUPPLIER	PLANTING POSITION

PLANT NAME	WHERE SEEN

SUPPLIER	PLANTING POSITION

PLANT NAME	WHERE SEEN

SUPPLIER	PLANTING POSITION

PLANT NAME	WHERE SEEN

SUPPLIER	PLANTING POSITION

PLANT NAME	WHERE SEEN

SUPPLIER	PLANTING POSITION

PLANT NAME	WHERE SEEN

SUPPLIER	PLANTING POSITION

PLANT NAME	WHERE SEEN

SUPPLIER	PLANTING POSITION

ROSES

PLANT NAME	WHERE SEEN

SUPPLIER	PLANTING POSITION

PLANT NAME	WHERE SEEN

SUPPLIER	PLANTING POSITION

PLANT NAME	WHERE SEEN

SUPPLIER	PLANTING POSITION

PLANT NAME	WHERE SEEN

SUPPLIER	PLANTING POSITION

PLANT NAME	WHERE SEEN

SUPPLIER	PLANTING POSITION

CLIMBERS

PLANT NAME	WHERE SEEN

SUPPLIER PLANTING POSITION

PLANT NAME	WHERE SEEN

SUPPLIER	PLANTING POSITION

PLANT NAME	WHERE SEEN

SUPPLIER	PLANTING POSITION

PLANT NAME	WHERE SEEN

SUPPLIER	PLANTING POSITION

PLANT NAME	WHERE SEEN

SUPPLIER	PLANTING POSITION

PERENNIALS

PLANT NAME	WHERE SEEN

SUPPLIER	PLANTING POSITION

PLANT NAME	WHERE SEEN

SUPPLIER	PLANTING POSITION

PLANT NAME	WHERE SEEN

SUPPLIER	PLANTING POSITION

PLANT NAME	WHERE SEEN

SUPPLIER	PLANTING POSITION

PLANT NAME	WHERE SEEN

SUPPLIER	PLANTING POSITION

PLANT NAME	WHERE SEEN

SUPPLIER	PLANTING POSITION

PLANT NAME	WHERE SEEN

SUPPLIER	PLANTING POSITION

PLANT NAME	WHERE SEEN

SUPPLIER	PLANTING POSITION

PLANT NAME	WHERE SEEN

SUPPLIER	PLANTING POSITION

BULBS

PLANT NAME	WHERE SEEN

SUPPLIER	PLANTING POSITION

PLANT NAME	WHERE SEEN

SUPPLIER	PLANTING POSITION

PLANT NAME	WHERE SEEN

SUPPLIER	PLANTING POSITION

PLANT NAME	WHERE SEEN

SUPPLIER	PLANTING POSITION

PLANT NAME	WHERE SEEN

SUPPLIER	PLANTING POSITION

ANNUALS & BIENNIALS

ANNUALS & BIENNIALS

PLANT NAME	WHERE SEEN

SUPPLIER	PLANTING POSITION

PLANT NAME	WHERE SEEN

SUPPLIER	PLANTING POSITION

PLANT NAME	WHERE SEEN

SUPPLIER	PLANTING POSITION

PLANT NAME	WHERE SEEN

SUPPLIER	PLANTING POSITION

PLANT NAME	WHERE SEEN

SUPPLIER	PLANTING POSITION

SPECIAL INTEREST

SPECIAL INTEREST

PLANT NAME	WHERE SEEN

SUPPLIER	PLANTING POSITION

PLANT NAME	WHERE SEEN

SUPPLIER	PLANTING POSITION

PLANT NAME	WHERE SEEN

SUPPLIER	PLANTING POSITION

PLANT NAME	WHERE SEEN

SUPPLIER	PLANTING POSITION

PLANT NAME	WHERE SEEN

SUPPLIER	PLANTING POSITION

Frances Lincoln Limited
www.franceslincoln.com

The Royal Horticultural Society Plant Notebook (White)
Copyright © Frances Lincoln Limited 2013
Text and illustrations copyright © the Royal Horticultural Society 2013 and printed under licence granted by the Royal Horticultural Society, Registered Charity number 222879/SC038262.
For more information visit our website or call 0845 130 4646
An interest in gardening is all you need to enjoy being a member of the RHS. Website: www.rhs.org.uk

First Frances Lincoln edition 2013

All rights reserved. No part of this publication may be reproduced, stored in a retrieval system or transmitted, in any form, or by any means, electronic, mechanical, photocopying, recording or otherwise, without either prior permission in writing from the publishers or a licence permitting restricted copying. In the United Kingdom such licences are issued by the Copyright Licensing Agency, Saffron House, 6–10 Kirby Street, London EC1N 8TS.

All the images are taken from the collection held at the Royal Horticultural Library's Lindley Library and are copyright the Royal Horticultural Society

Designed by Arianna Osti

A catalogue record for this book is available from the British Library
ISBN: 978-0-7112-3445-1
Printed in China

9 8 7 6 5 4 3 2 1

Also available:
The Royal Horticultural Society Plant Notebook (Blue) 978-0-7112-3418-5
The Royal Horticultural Society Plant Notebook (Yellow) 978-0-7112-3446-8